One day, a century or so from now, some historian will gather up the many works published over the last thirty years by the Educational Division of the Superintendent's Office in Via della Ninna, Florence. Looking at such body of work, our hypothetical researcher will not be able to escape the fact that, if any societal education and acculturation service has come out of the Florentine Superintendence between the 20th and 21st centuries, that service has without a doubt been rendered by its women art historians, to wit, Maria Fossi Todorow, Maria Grazia Trenti Antonelli and Maria Paola Masini, the three successive directors of the Florentine Educational Division since its inception. One of them, Maria Grazia Trenti Antonelli, is the author of this book devoted to frescoing, which I have the honour of introducing here.

Over the last thirty years the Superintendent's Office has produced hundreds of exhibition catalogues, collections, area studies and scientific publications of every sort. However (putting myself in the shoes of our hypothetical future historian), only the svelte publications of the Educational Division have ever sought to impart understanding and appreciation of art, not only to schoolchildren, but also to the public at large, to the 'museum crowd'.

In this book the author deals with frescoing, the prince of all Medieval and Renaissance pictorial techniques. It does so by envisaging a dialogue between Beato Angelico and his student, Benozzo Gozzoli, in the Florentine Church of San Marco. We are therefore dealing with reality, because San Marco is a public museum and the frescoes there are indeed the work of this master and his pupil. Then, departing from reality (to be effective, teaching must proceed by exemplification, and the examples must be concretely verifiable and understandable to all), the author goes on to provide a clear, methodical, yet all but tiresome, description of the techniques involved in frescoing, techniques to translate idea into drawing, drawing into sinopia, wall into surface preparation and, finally, the entire succession of operations followed to achieve that marvel of air-dried mineral colouring that is the 'good fresco' in the Florentine tradition.

This is all presented by Trenti Antonelli so clearly and in such an appealing way that at the dialogue's end, no one, not even university art history students (to whom the book is highly recommended), will ever be able to forget the techniques of frescoing. Here is a perfect example of educational service, of truly participatory culture on offer to society. In addition to the heartfelt gratitude of the Superintendent's Office to our dear friend and colleague, Trenti Antonelli, I wish to offer my sincere wish (which is also a working commitment) that the new director of the Educational Division, Maria Paola Masini, continue in this fruitful, virtuous line of laudable publications.

Antonio Paolucci

Soprintendente per il Polo Museale Fiorentino

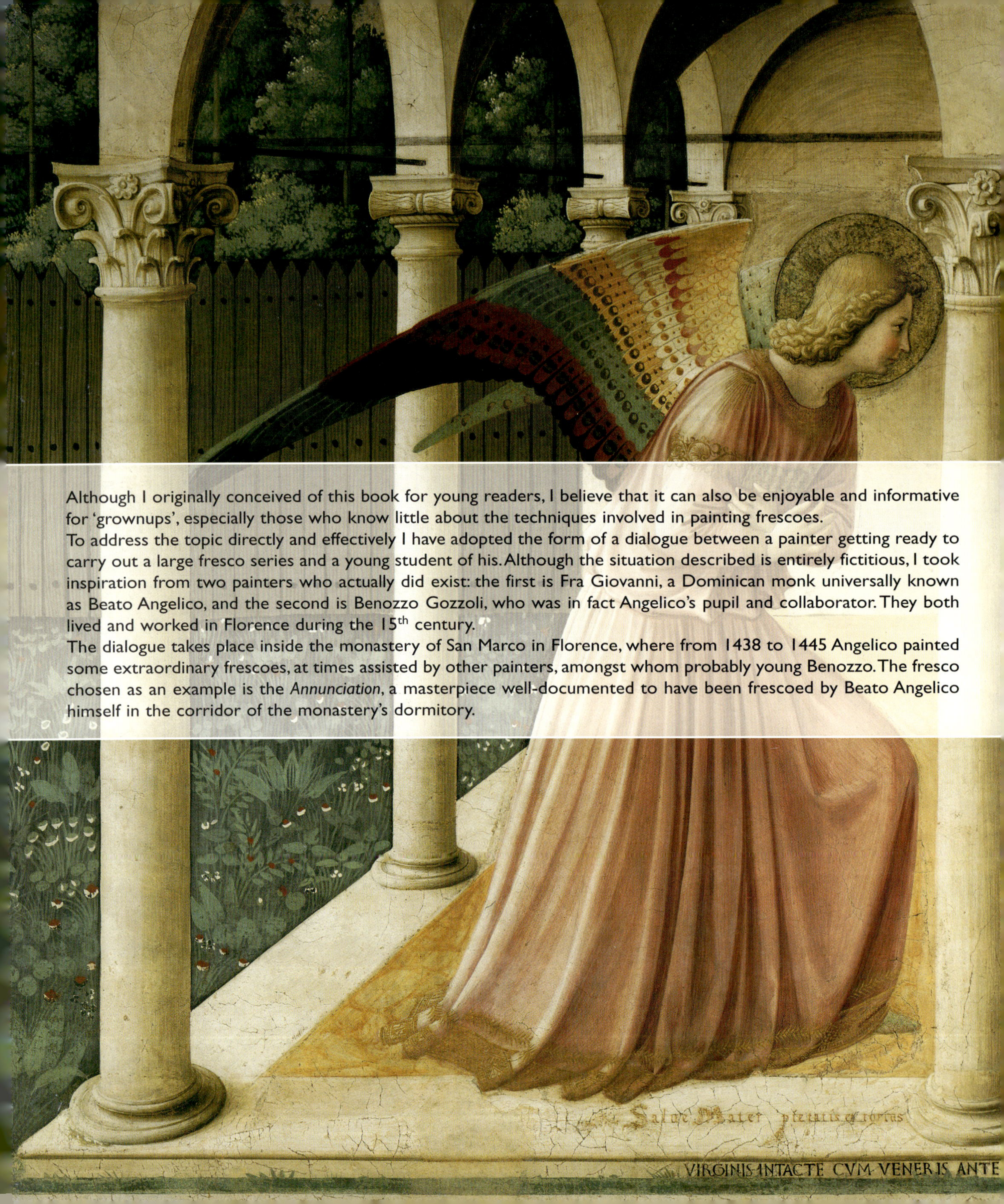


Although I originally conceived of this book for young readers, I believe that it can also be enjoyable and informative for 'grownups', especially those who know little about the techniques involved in painting frescoes.
To address the topic directly and effectively I have adopted the form of a dialogue between a painter getting ready to carry out a large fresco series and a young student of his. Although the situation described is entirely fictitious, I took inspiration from two painters who actually did exist: the first is Fra Giovanni, a Dominican monk universally known as Beato Angelico, and the second is Benozzo Gozzoli, who was in fact Angelico's pupil and collaborator. They both lived and worked in Florence during the 15th century.
The dialogue takes place inside the monastery of San Marco in Florence, where from 1438 to 1445 Angelico painted some extraordinary frescoes, at times assisted by other painters, amongst whom probably young Benozzo. The fresco chosen as an example is the *Annunciation*, a masterpiece well-documented to have been frescoed by Beato Angelico himself in the corridor of the monastery's dormitory.

# PREPARING THE WALL: THE *ARRICCIO*

**FRA GIOVANNI**

Come Benozzo, I shall show you all the walls to be frescoed. The Dominican monks for whom this monastery was built wish to have sacred images in all the rooms of their dormitory here. They have also asked me to decorate the corridor with objects of their devotion. [1]

BENOZZO

Maestro, there are so many rooms! This is going to be a long task indeed!

That is why I need you, dear Benozzo! Have the mason boys help you and begin plastering all the surfaces to be frescoed. In the meantime, I will prepare the drawings.

*Some months later*

Maestro, come and see, I hope that you are pleased with my work. I prepared the mortar for the plaster by mixing sifted sand with lime and water, always taking care to use one part mortar to two parts sand. I waited a few days, then started to spread the lime paste over the wall. I applied it to the surface unevenly, so that it wouldn't turn out too smooth, but somewhat rough, '*arricciato*', you know, 'curled'. The plaster has dried perfectly in this beautiful weather, and it is all ready to start working on, whenever you wish.



**LIME**

1 Mixing lime, that is, calcium oxide, with water causes a chemical reaction that forms calcium hydroxide, a process called 'slaking'. The reaction takes a few days to complete, after which the resulting lime mortar or plaster can be spread over the wall. The surface must be left rough, so that the second coat of plaster (called the 'intonaco') adheres better. For this reason, Italians called this first layer the 'arriccio' or curled surface. In English it is also called the 'brown coat'.

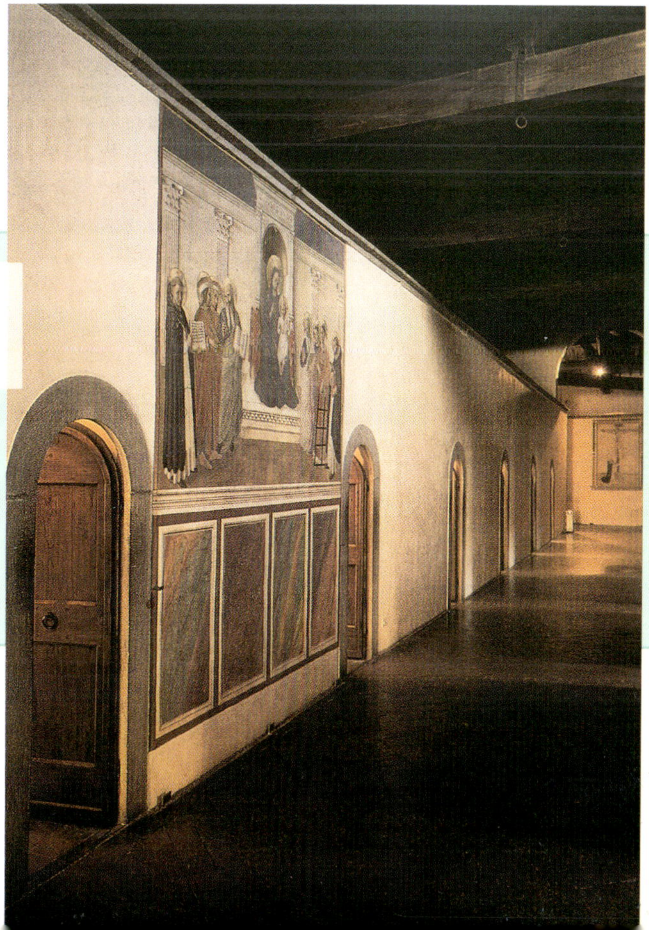

A corridor in the Monastery of San Marco

## THE PREPARATORY DRAWING OR SINOPIA

**FRA GIOVANNI**

Good.
Now I'll show you how to create a fresco. You see this corridor here? I am going to decorate it with a representation of the Annunciation. I'll begin by preparing the painting surface by tracing the vertical and horizontal reference lines. This will make my work easier.

*The next day*

BENOZZO

Maestro, I observed everything you did very carefully. Using a length of twine, first you measured the width of the wall and found the midway point, where you attached a plumb line with a nail to get a perpendicular vertical line to the floor. Then you used a **'corda da battere'** to clearly mark the line on the wall, and with a large compass you drew two semicircles to trace a horizontal line parallel to the floor. [2]

Bravo Benozzo! I see that you are a fast learner. Now I can start transferring my drawings onto the wall.

Maestro, watching you work leaves me totally in awe. You draw the charcoal sketches freehanded, with such quick, sure strokes!

I must admit, I am comfortable with the traditional techniques. Watch carefully as the drawing emerges on the wall. Firstly, I make a quick charcoal outline, which can be easily erased if I want to make any corrections. Then I use a brush dipped in light-coloured ochre to trace the contours of the black lines, and lastly wipe away the initial charcoal drawing with some paintbrushes. At this point, I go over everything once again with **red sinopia** in order to make it stand out more, and lastly finish up the figures and add shading. [3]

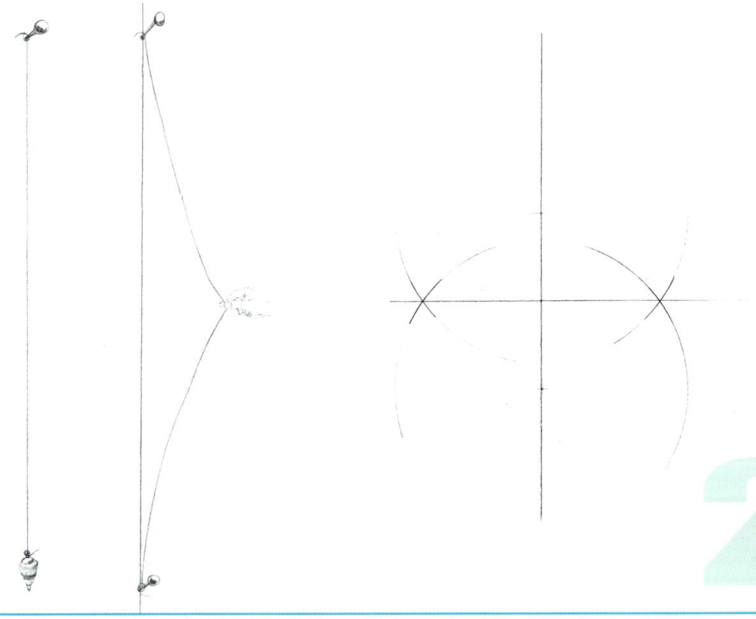

2

### CORDA DA BATTERE

To trace these basic reference lines, artists used a string, similar to modern-day chalk lines, which they kept in a pouch full of coloured powder (the red-coloured ochre pigment, called sinopia or charcoal). The string was tensed between two nails securing its ends and then plucked, so it 'beat' (i.e., battere) against the wall, leaving a coloured line.

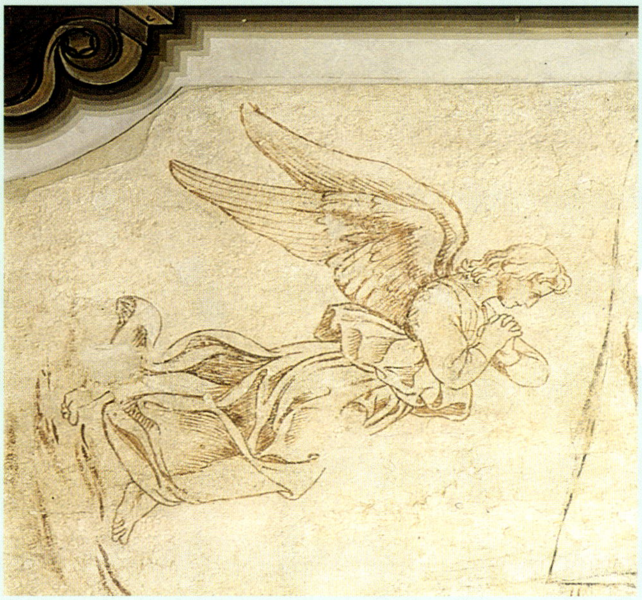

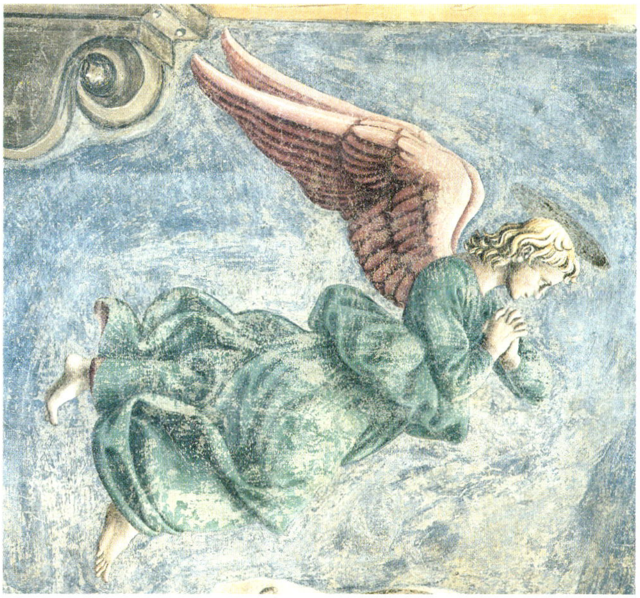

# 3 SINOPIA

The technique illustrated by Fra Giovanni has been described in detail in the *Book of Art*, by Cennino Cennini, a painter who lived in the late 14th century. We have good reason to believe that Beato Angelico followed the same procedure.

The preparatory drawing that the painter sketched out on the rough 'arriccio' surface is called a **sinopia**, named for the red earth pigment used to draw it.

Today we have many sinopias of age-old frescoes that had to be detached from their walls because this was the only way the artwork could be conserved.



Andrea del Castagno, *Crucifixion*, detail of the *Mourning Angels*, sinopia and fresco. Florence, Cenacolo di Sant'Apollonia.

BENOZZO

FRA GIOVANNI

*The next day*

Such a beautiful drawing! I cannot help but marvel at the sinopia that you made on the arriccio. What a pity that it will soon disappear forever, covered by the new coat of plaster.

T'is a pity, t'is true, but that will take a while, won't it? We must proceed bit by bit. You know that painting '*a fresco*' means doing it 'on fresh' plaster. So the finishing coat, the '*intonaco*', needs to be applied a little at a time, just enough for a day's work. Have you prepared the plaster for the new coat?

Yes, Maestro. I made it myself – half lime and half sand. It is so fine that it looks like cream.

Today I am going to paint the entire upper portion of the fresco. Help me apply a plaster layer and make sure that it is perfectly smooth. Oh, and don't forget to leave a 'scarped' border, that is, a sloping edge where we can join tomorrow's coat.

There, I've finished, Maestro. Why don't you start painting now?

It is best to wait about two hours – the plaster is too damp now. When it is ready I will have to work quickly to catch that magic moment when you can sense the plaster thickening.

What happens when you paint on still damp plaster?

No one knows exactly, but experience teaches me that when the plaster dries it absorbs the paint, and the surface comes out looking like coloured marble. [4] Meanwhile, let's go and get the cartoons in my study.

The finishing coat of plaster (called 'intonaco') on which the artist painted 'a fresco' (literally, 'on fresh') was made of **lime and sand in equal proportions**, mixed thoroughly so that it would form a smoother surface than the rough, underlying brown coat or 'arriccio'.



INTONACO

## PITTURA "A FRESCO"

Today, we do know what happens when an artist paints on freshly laid plaster:as the slaked lime in the plaster dries, it combines with carbon dioxide in the air to produce a film of calcium carbonate **(carbonatation process)**, which covers the pigment particles to give that marbly appearance Fra Giovanni speaks of.

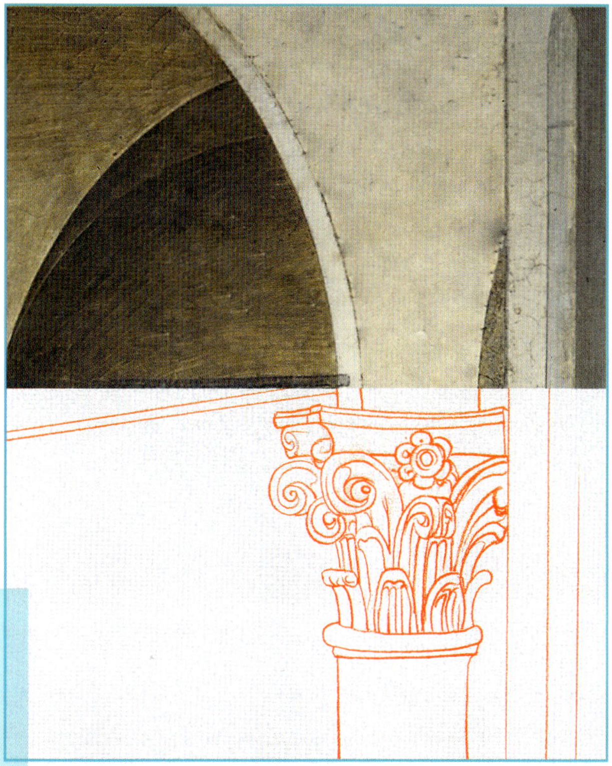

# 4

The artist paints downward, from top to bottom. For each day's work he plasters over a part of the sinopia with the **intonaco**; the size of the area depends on how difficult the subject to be painted is: the harder the painting, the smaller the area. After redrawing the plastered-over sketch, he begins applying the paint, well knowing that he must complete the day's work before the plaster dries!

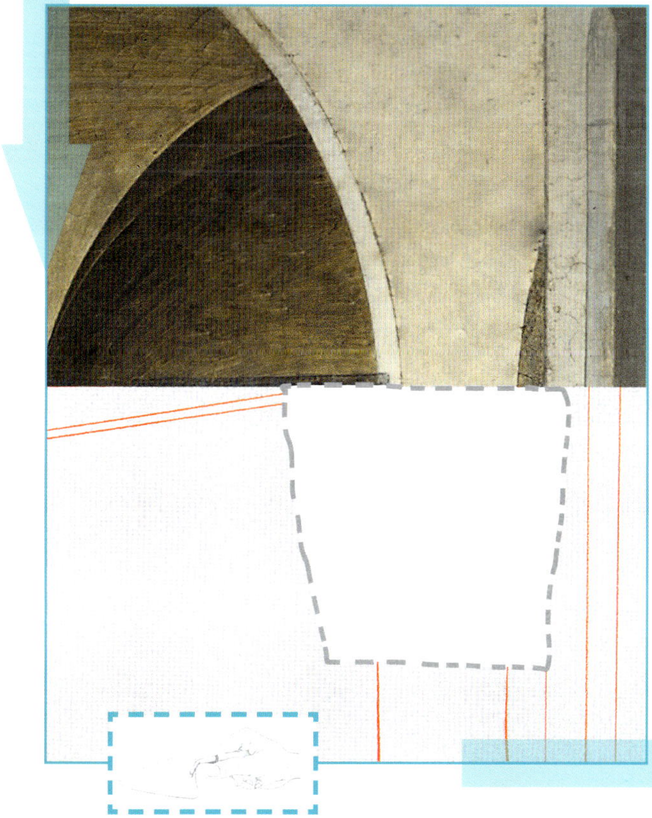

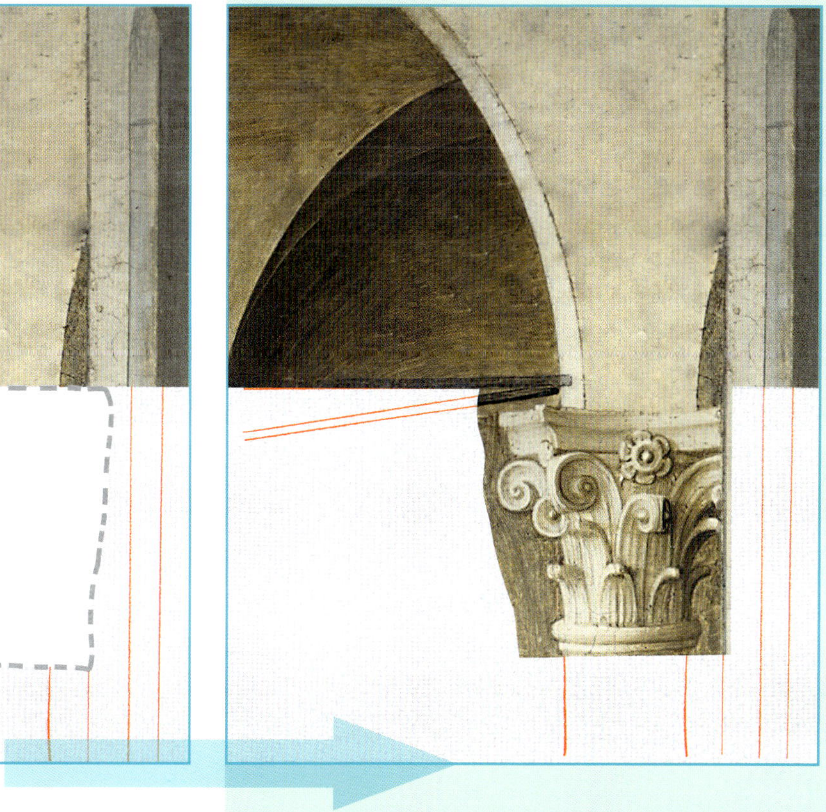

# THE CARTOON AND POUNCING

## FRA GIOVANNI

You see all these sheets, Benozzo? There are so many drawings because they often portray only some particular detail: a head, perhaps, the folds of a garment, an angel's wings or the figure of a mason boy whose portrait I drew here from life while he was working or resting. All these sketches help me to make a preparatory drawing for the fresco. That drawing serves as a guide for me to trace the sinopia on the wall and then to execute the fresco itself. I sometimes need to enlarge portions of the drawing to the true dimensions of the fresco. Do you see that large **cartoon** that I have just made? Get it. Now, we just hold it up against the fresh plaster and go over all the lines with an awl.
What do you think will happen?

## BENOZZO

The outline of the drawing will be etched into the wall and it will be easier for you to copy that part of the sinopia covered by the new layer of plaster. [5]
Maestro, I've heard that some other masters use a technique called bouncing to transfer their drawings onto the fresh plaster.

My dear Benozzo, that's **pouncing**, not bouncing! Yes, one could use pouncing to transfer the drawings. Do you know exactly how it is done?

No, but once I saw a young apprentice, like me, busy making lots of small holes in a drawing. I'm still wondering what the purpose of that was.

Here, I'll show you. Take that drawing on the table there; it already has perforations – those small holes you speak of – all along its contours. Hold it up against the wall. Now, pick up that pad full of charcoal powder and pat it hard along the perforated lines. Have you got them all? Good, now remove the sheet. What do you see?



Maestro, the coal has passed through the holes and left a trace on the wall. [6]

Now, take this stick of charcoal and go over all of it again.

Amazing! I've copied your drawing, exactly the same!

I believe that the plaster is ready. Today I am going to do a rather large portion, but it is an easy one. I am going to start by applying the paint, diluted in water, with a thin brush.

## LO SPOLVERO

The second technique described by Fra Giovanni for transferring the drawings onto freshly laid plaster is called **'pouncing'**. We know that it was used to decorate walls since the 14th century. However, the frescoes at San Marco show no evidence of its application.

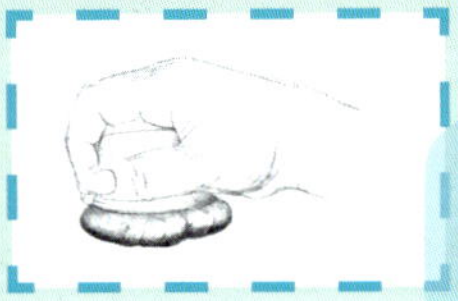

6

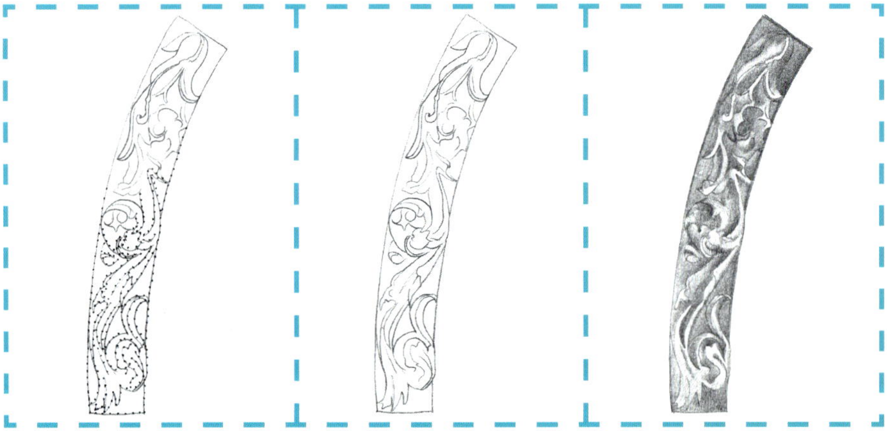

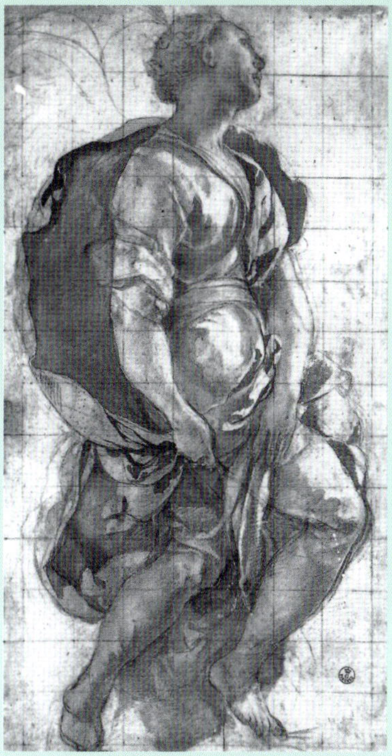

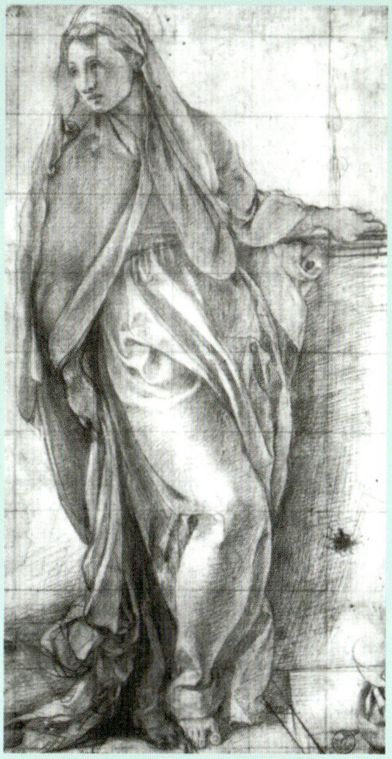

# THE CARTOON

Fra Angelico used the technique of etching to trace the outlines of Mary's mantle and the architecture in the fresco of the *Annunciation*.
This technique, already in use during the 15th century, became ever more widespread in the early 16th century. The **cartoon** was obtained by enlarging a small-scale, preliminary sketch via the technique called 'squaring'. The small drawing was divided into many squares, then a cartoon as large as the finished work was also divided into the same number of squares. In this way, it became easy to transfer the entire drawing, by enlarging each detail contained in the single squares, one by one. The images here show two drawings by Pontormo, together with the frescoes they were made for; they were prepared and enlarged through the technique of squaring.

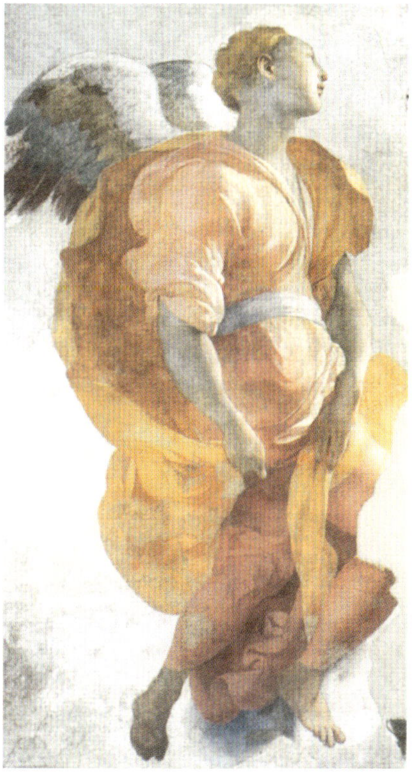

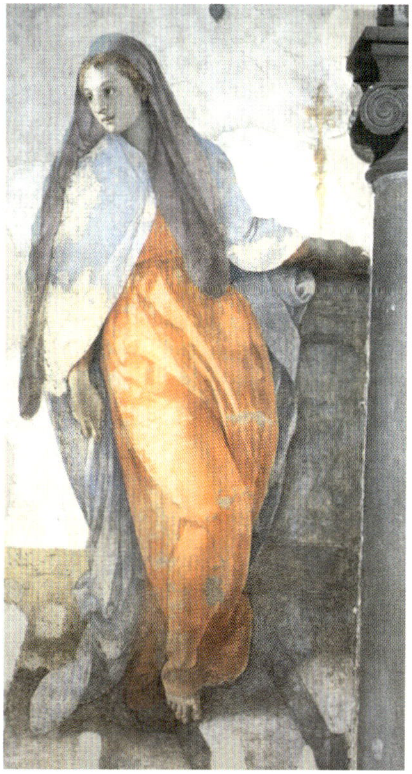

Pontormo, *Virgin Mary* and the *Angel of the Annunciation*, studies for the fresco in the Capponi Chapel. Florence, Gabinetto Disegni e Stampe degli Uffizi, no. 6653 F and no. 448 F

Pontormo, *Annunciation*. Florence, Santa Felicita

# ANOTHER 'DAY'

BENOZZO

**FRA GIOVANNI**

*A few days later*

Maestro, the fresh plaster coat is ready. I was careful to join it seamlessly with yesterday's layer. But I must admit, I just hated having to cover the beautiful head of the Archangel Gabriel. You will be able to duplicate it exactly, won't you?

Of course. Here, you see? First I redraw the contours with the verdaccio and then go on to shape the face with the verdeterra.

While I work on this, you prepare three jars of the paints I'll need for the skin colouring. Mix some white 'bianco sangiovanni' with different amounts of red ochre, so that you get three shades: light, medium and dark. Later I'll use the pure white for the eyes, some black for the contours, and red to paint the lips and for some touches on the cheeks. For the angel's blonde hair, I'll need a light ochre to start with, then a darker shade for the parts in shadow, and lastly a touch of white to highlight his locks.

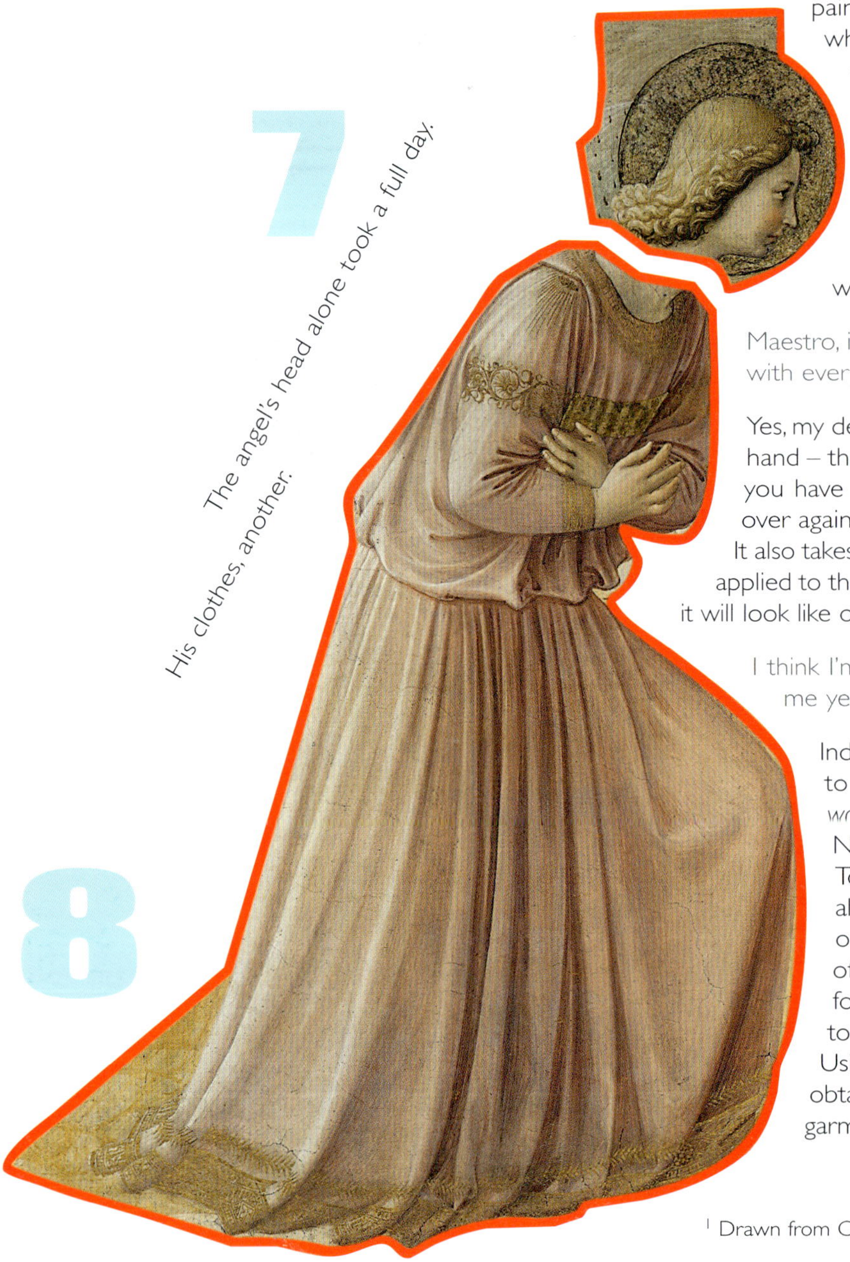

7

The angel's head alone took a full day.
His clothes, another.

8

Maestro, it's amazing to see the angel's head come to life with every stroke of your brush! [7]

Yes, my dear Benozzo, the fresco painter must have a sure hand – there is no margin for error. If you make a mistake, you have to wipe out an entire day's work and start all over again the next.

It also takes great experience, because when the paint is first applied to the fresh plaster its hue is quite different from what it will look like once the plaster has dried.

I think I'm beginning to get the idea – it is going to take me years to learn to paint frescoes!

Indeed, but they will be years well spent, because to work the wall *"is the sweetest and most elegant work there is"* [1]

Now, enough chatter!

Tomorrow I am going to do the archangel's robes, all pink. [8] I need some jars of different shades of pink. With the pure pigment I'll paint the parts of the folds in shadow and use the lighter shades for the more salient parts. And now... just a few touches of white will highlight the more sunlit areas. Using different colour gradations will enable me to obtain a lifelike depiction of the folds of the angel's garments, as if Gabriel had just alighted on earth.

[1] Drawn from Cennino Cennini's *Libro dell'arte (Book of Art)*, Chapter LXVII.

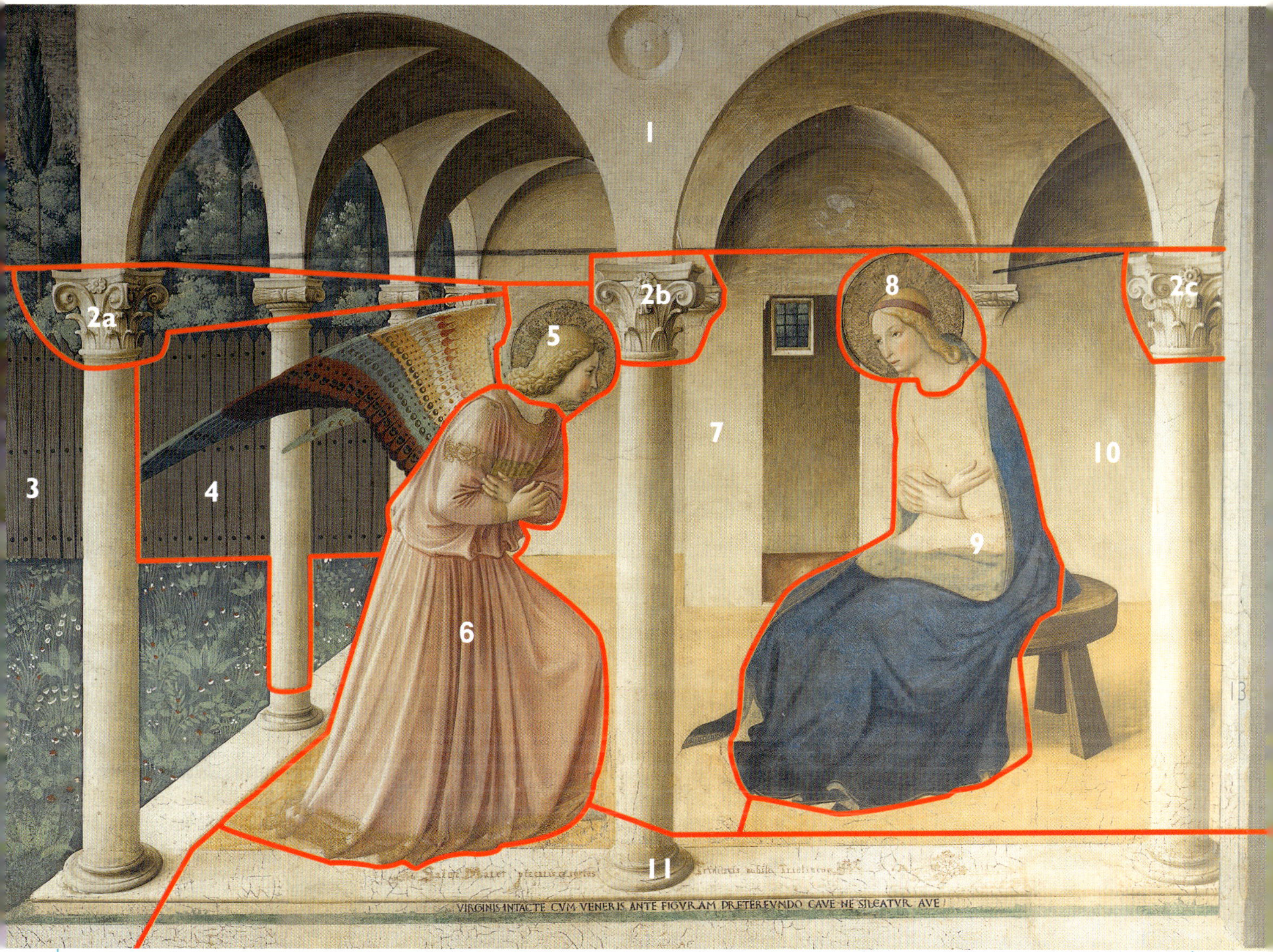


Today we can still distinguish the different **days** of a fresco's execution by carefully observing the seams in the plaster coat. Beato Angelico's technique was so perfect that at times it is quite difficult to make out such seams.

# PAINTING 'DRY' ON THE WALL

BENOZZO

**FRA GIOVANNI**

*A few days later*

Maestro I have spent hours looking at your angel and I never tire of it.
His wings – they are fantastic! [9]

It's not finished yet. Today I am going to put the gold on his halo.
As you know, we painters use gold leaf for such work. First, the surface to be gilded must be coated with a binder, which is a sort of glue, and then the gold leaf applied and pressed down hard with the palm of your hand. Now pay attention, because I also want to decorate the angel's robes. too. To do this, I take some gold dust, bind it with tempera and brush it on like paint for the embroidery of his robe. [10]

I don't understand. You are working on dry plaster. Didn't you warn me always to finish the work the same day, while the plaster was still damp?

Well, the time has come to tell you that this is not always true.

How so?

Some pigments are not really suited for wall painting, others can be used, but only on dry plaster, and only after mixing in tempera to bind them.
There are two types of tempera that can be used: one made with whole eggs mixed with latex, which is a residue extracted from fig-tree twigs and leaves; the other is made with egg yolks alone.
Tomorrow I'll teach you some new techniques using tempera.



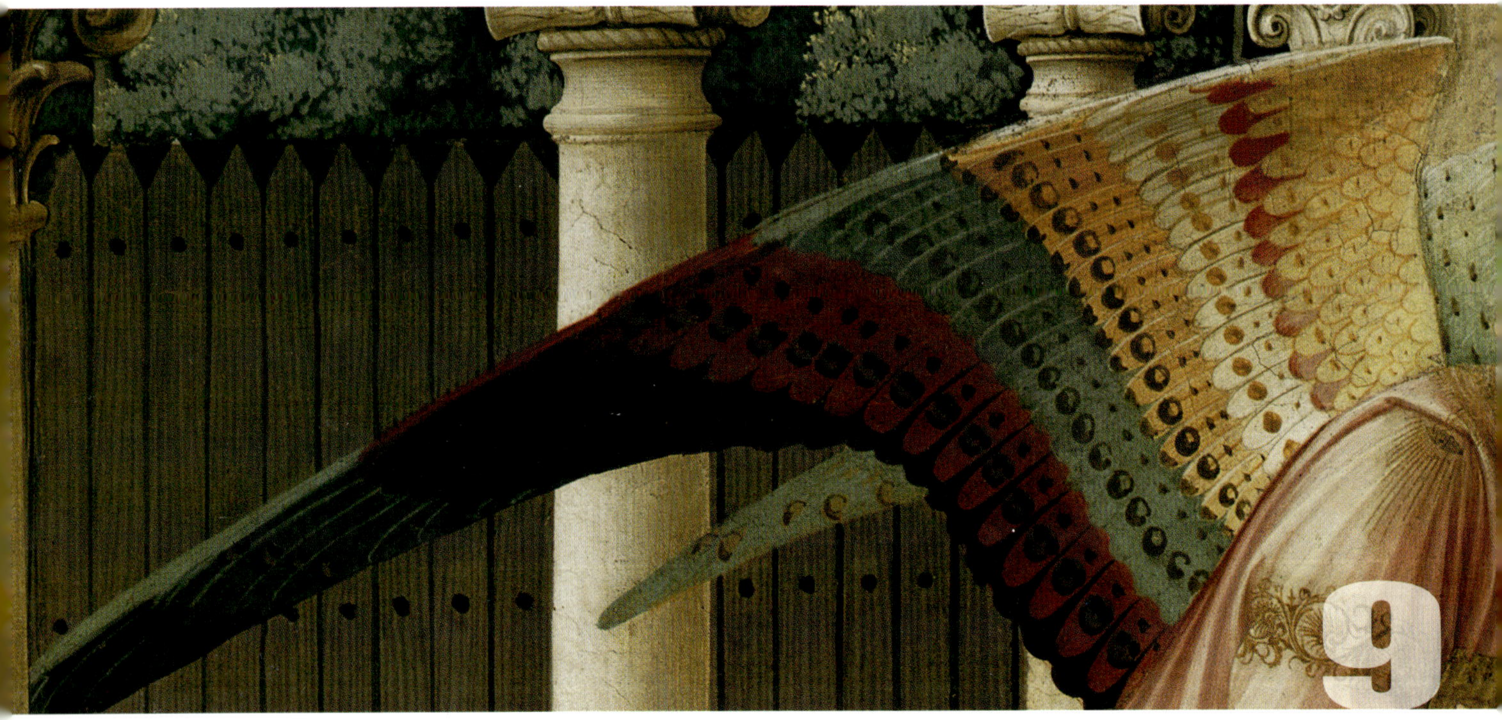

9

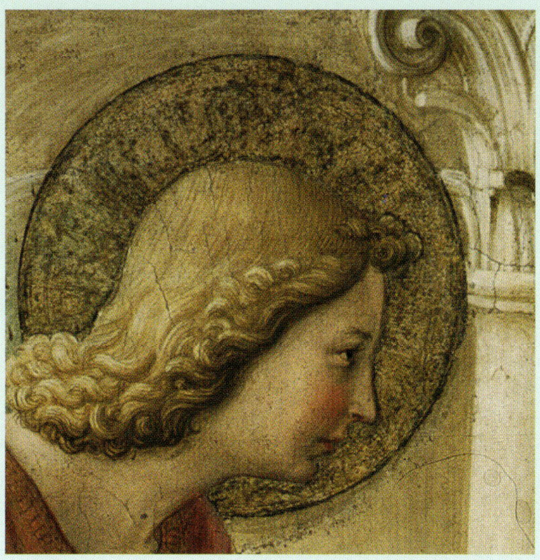

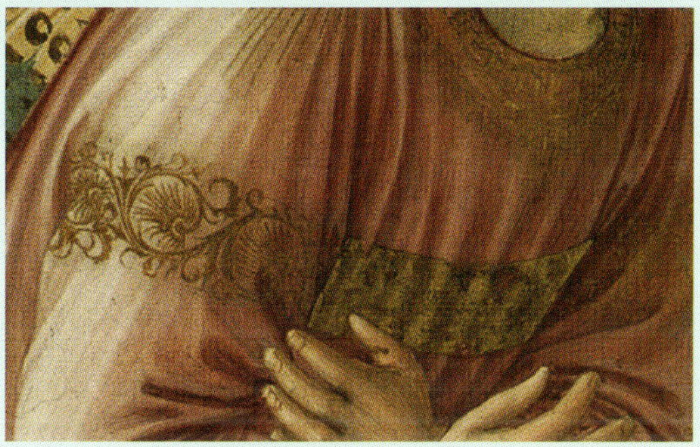

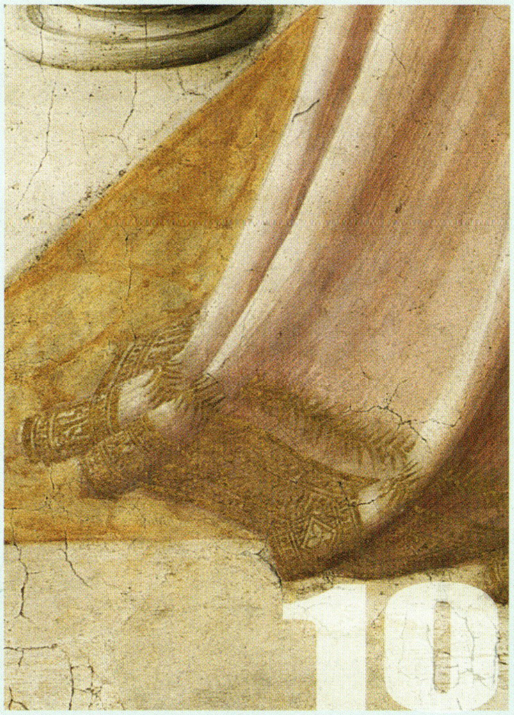
10

*A few days later*

BENOZZO

**FRA GIOVANNI**

Maestro, the Virgin Mary is absolutely breathtaking! [11]
What paints shall I prepare for her mantle?

I'll need the red haematite as a base for the blue. Then get some azurite from that cupboard there. You should know that both the blue pigments, azurite and ultramarine, are very expensive, so I keep them under lock and key with the gold. I have discussed it with the prior of the monastery and we've decided to use them only here in the ground floor hallway, in the communal spaces. Certain luxuries are unsuitable for a monk's cell.

Maestro, what need I do to get the various blue tones with azurite?

You use another white pigment, called biacca, made from lead.

If I understand correctly, the colours applied to fresh plaster become embedded in it. Instead, the ones placed on the dry surface are simply stuck to it with the tempera, which is a kind of glue. Isn't there the risk that over time these tempera pigments can detach and ruin the painting?

That is a good question. Yes, it is true, while the fresco can withstand rain and inclement weather, the portions done 'dry' are much more delicate and in time may decay. [12]



11

12

In the large *Crucifixion* in the San Marco Chapter House large portions of the sky, which Beato Angelico painted with **azurite**, are missing, only the dark red colour of the preparatory drawing remains.

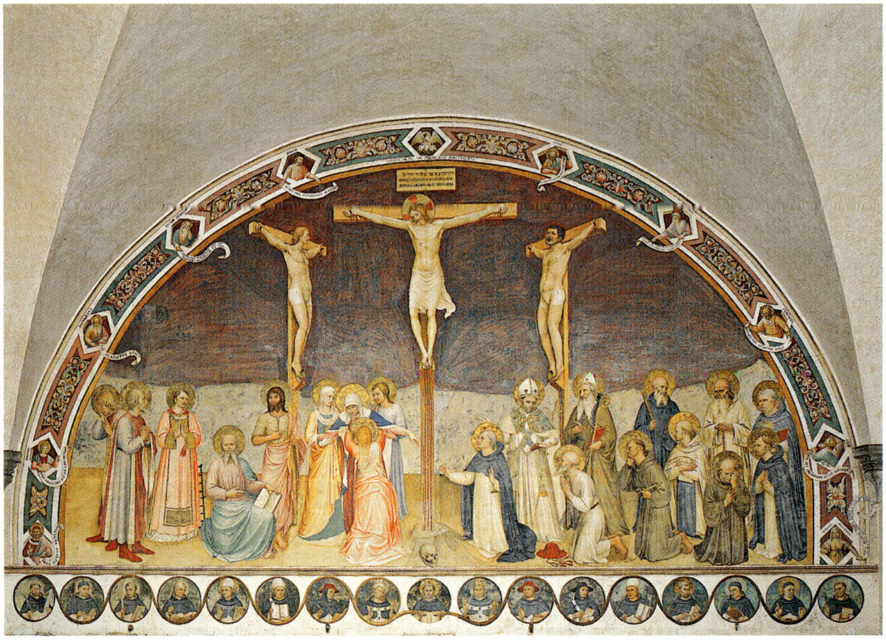

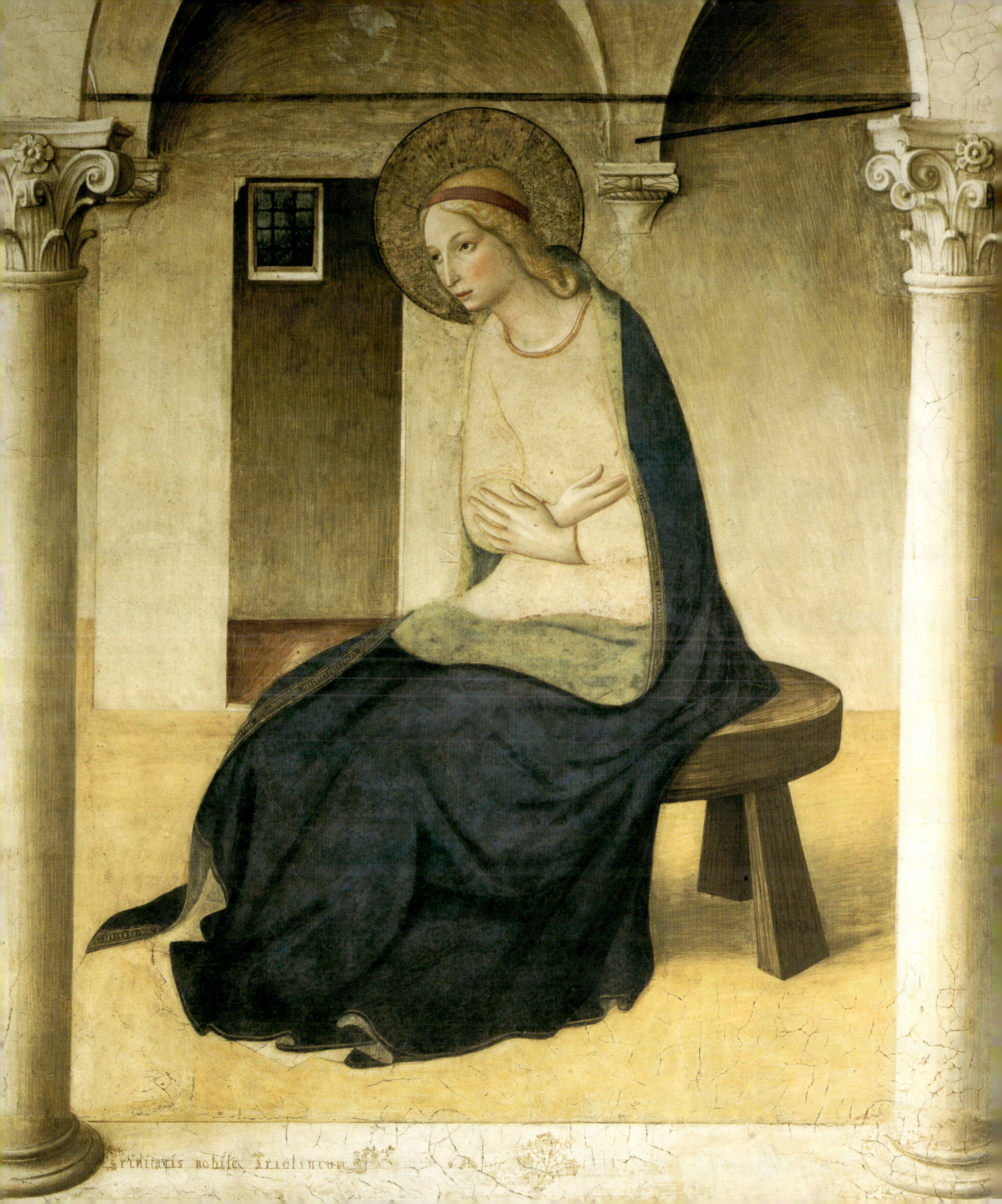
Trinitatis nobile Triclinium

*A few days later*

**FRA GIOVANNI** The fresco of the *Annunciation* is almost complete. Only the left-hand portion above the portico columns remains to be finished. I have already painted the fence and a dark background above and below. Now I'll complete it on the dry surface of the upper portion by adding some trees with various green pigments, using bianco sangiovanni as binder.
In the lower part here, instead, I'll paint a flowering field. All I need do is to add some thickly applied touches of white and red pigment just above the green tufts of the leaves. See what a great effect that produces!? [13]

BENOZZO Maestro, it truly looks like a corner of paradise!



13

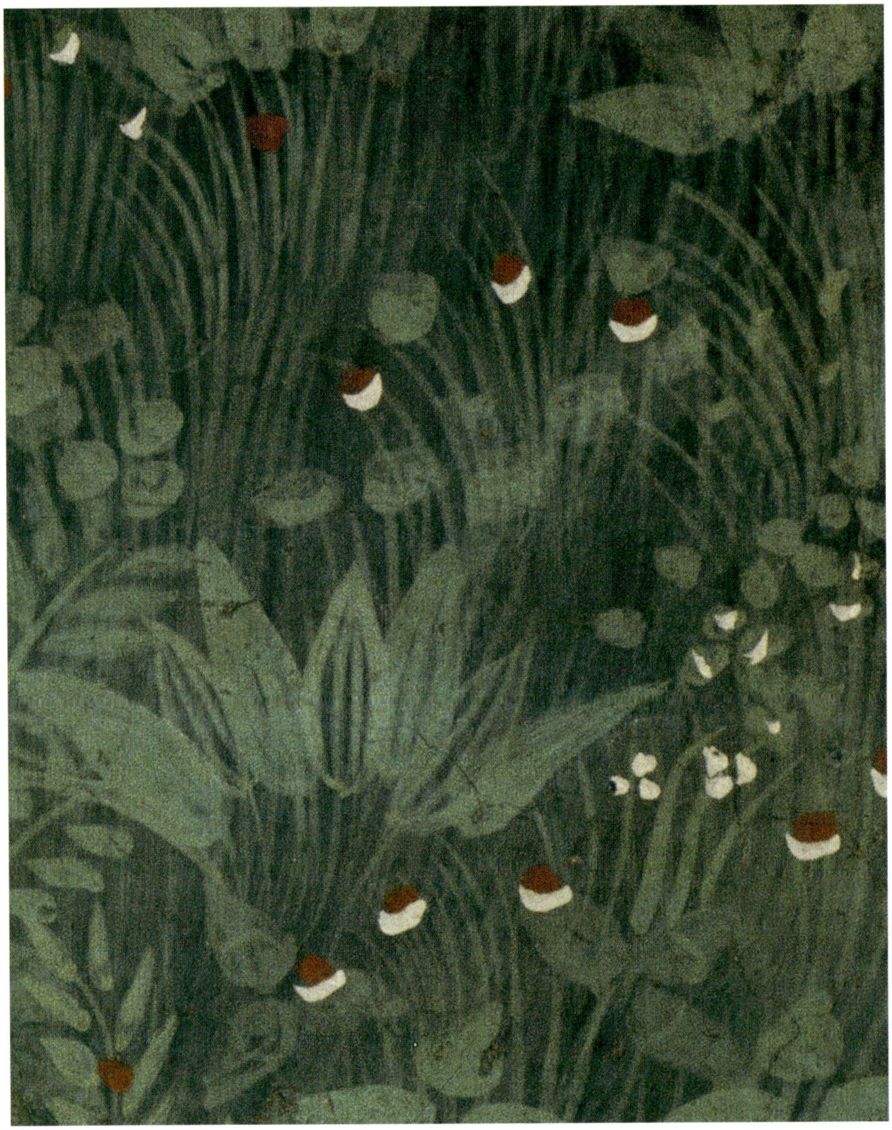

# COLOURING MATERIALS USED IN FRESCOES

**White:** *bianco sangiovanni*, made with lime, and the lead-based *biacca*.

**Black:** three types of black were known: *smoke-* or *lamp-black*, obtained by burning linseed oil; *sarment* or *vine-shoot charcoal;* and *charcoal from almond shells and peach pits*.

**Yellow:** *giallorino*, also know as *Naples yellow*, a lead-based pigment obtained artificially.

**Red:** obtained from various types of *ochre*, that is, natural earth pigments that vary in colour from yellow, to red, orange-red and brown, depending on the iron content.

Mixing *sinopia* and *bianco sangiovanni* yielded *cinabrese,* similar in colour to cinnabar or vermilion.

*Sinopia* was a reddish ochre, already known centuries earlier, which got its name from the ancient city of Sinopia in Pontus on the Black Sea.

*Haematite,* the principal form of iron ore, was used to impart a beautiful dark red colour.

**Green:** *verdeterra* (literally, green earth) was obtained by grinding a clayey iron-rich mineral.

*Malachite*, also known as *mountain green*, is a semi-precious copper mineral, used on dry surfaces to obtain a brighter green.

Other green hues were made by mixing yellow and blue pigments.

**Blue:** *azurite,* also known as *azzurro della Magna* (i.e., German blue), was obtained from blue copper ore or copper carbonate, while *ultramarine* comes from the precious stone, lapis lazuli. Both were suitable only for dry surfaces. Other hues could also be obtained by mixing *indigo* with *bianco sangiovanni*.

**Indigo:** a pigment extracted from the plant of the same name, was often used in mixtures with other paints.

**Violet:** obtained by mixing *indigo* and *amethyst*.

**Light grey:** obtained by mixing *bianco sangiovanni* and *black*.

**Dark grey:** obtained by mixing *black* and *ochre*.

**Brown:** a mixture of *black*, *ochre* and *sinopia*.

# MASTER AND STUDENT

Let us now leave the young apprentice, Benozzo Bozzoli, to contemplate his Maestro's fresco, ever more eager to learn and take on such work himself.

In fact, Fra Giovanni's 'crash course' on the techniques of fresco painting has instilled him (and we hope the reader as well) with a great deal of enthusiasm.

But is this how things actually were? By a flight of fancy, let us journey back in time to pay a visit to a 14th or 15th-century Florentine art workshop.

What we would see would be the master artist, the Maestro, and some of his apprentices, all busy at various tasks. The youngest, even children as young as eight or nine years old, might be intent on drawing. In fact, young students were required to constantly make sketches from life or to copy the works of the great masters. [14]

Students also needed a good knowledge of the materials and tools of their trade. So, apprentices had to become intimately familiar with all products and utensils used in the shop.

During the first three years the parents of children accepted as workshop apprentices had to pay the shop's master to teach their children. Afterwards, it was the Maestro who paid a salary to the apprentices, because by now they were able to assist him in his work.

Apprentices lived and worked in their workshops for nine years, sometimes even longer. Clearly, it took a long time and a lot of effort indeed to become a good painter.

The dialogue between Fra Giovanni and Benozzo reveals the close, even affectionate relationship between them. The atmosphere in workshops must also have been quite family-like.

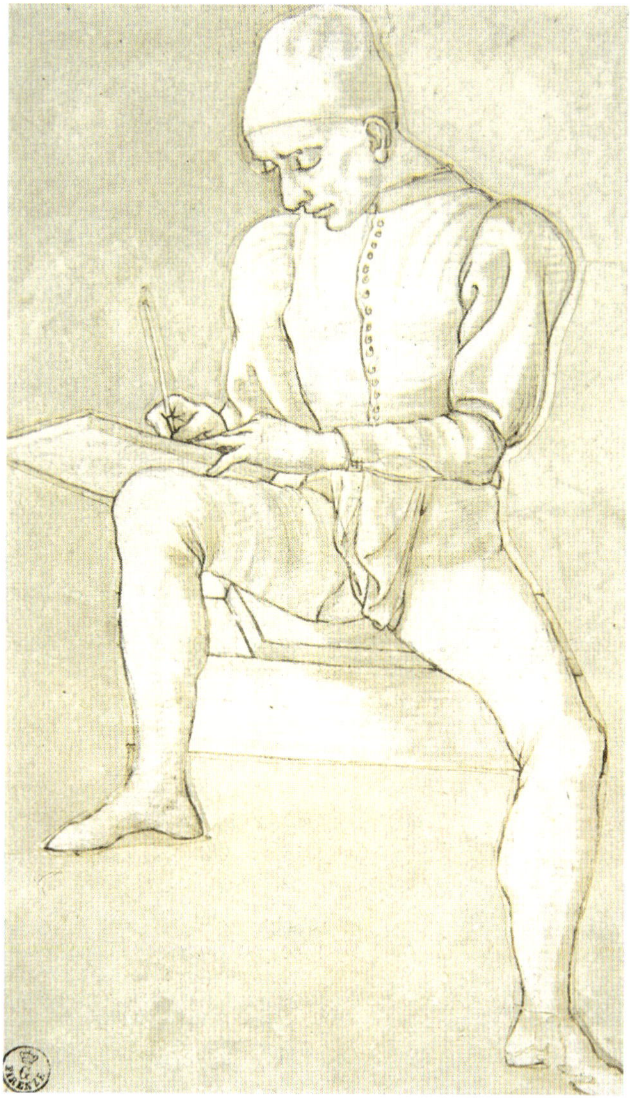

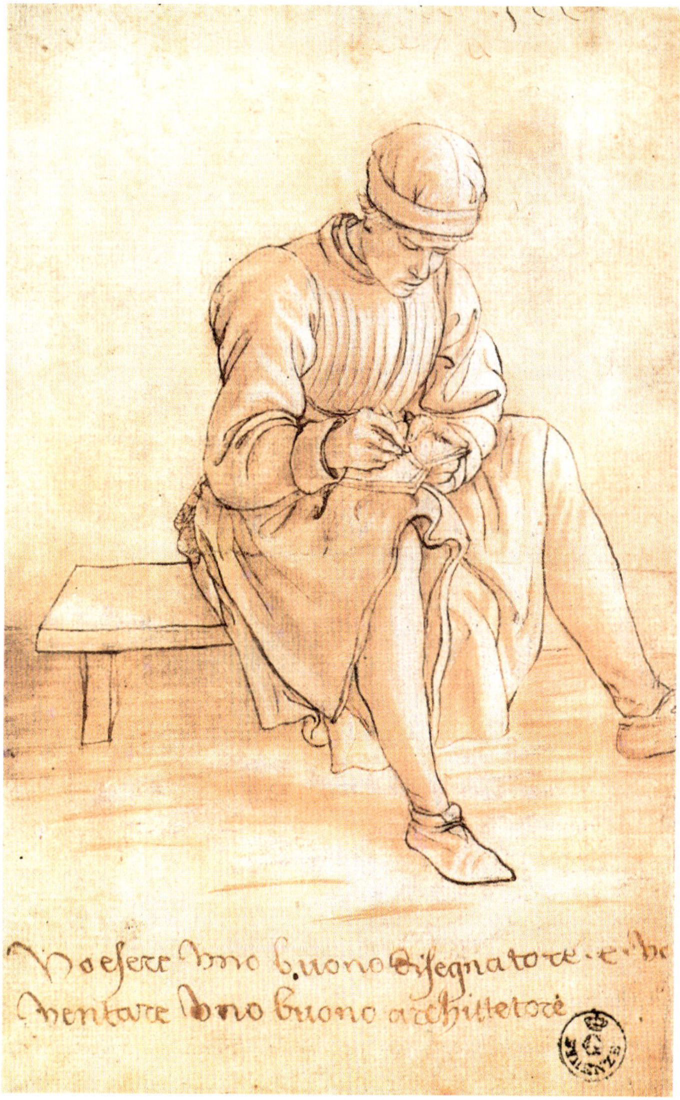



Maso Finiguerra, *Young man sitting and drawing.*
Florence, Gabinetto Disegni e Stampe degli Uffizi, no. 47 F

Maso Finiguerra, *Young man sitting and drawing.*
Florence, Gabinetto Disegni e Stampe degli Uffizi, no. 115 F

# SUMMING UP ...

A fresco is a wall painting executed by applying the colours '**a fresco**', that is on still 'fresh', damp plaster. First, a layer of plaster, obtained by mixing together water, mortar and sand, is spread out over the surface of the wall to be frescoed. This first layer must be left rather rough; for this reason it is called the '**arriccio**', or 'curled' surface.
After the plaster has dried, the painter traces the outlines of some preliminary sketches on the wall; these will serve as guides in executing the drawing. At this point, the artist starts drawing the subject he intends to portray directly on the wall, using red-coloured sinopia or black charcoal. This drawing is called the '**sinopia**', after the red ochre pigment most often used to make it.
Only now does the real painting begin. The artist must first decide how much of the preparatory drawing he can paint in one day. He then covers a suitable portion of the arriccio with a fresh layer of plaster, called the '**intonaco**', which must be perfectly smooth. After waiting for the plaster to set, so that it is best able to receive the colours, the painter starts painting, freehand, to redo that part of the sinopia that has been covered by the fresh intonaco.
The colours are mixed with water and applied to the plaster while it is still in the process of drying, so that the pigments are absorbed into it. This process of absorption only occurs while the plaster is still damp, so in a few hours the painter must complete the entire area covered by the fresh plaster. Each of these portions is called a **day** and can be recognized by the joints between the various days' work.
While hastening to paint the freshly plastered portion of the sinopia, the artist may at times see fit to exploit some helpful techniques. **Pouncing** enables the preliminary drawing to be transferred onto the wall by simply perforating the outlines of the drawing and then using a black powder-filled pad to mark the outlines on the plaster. Another often used technique is etching, by which the artist places a full-scale drawing of the fresco, called the **cartoon**, on the fresh plaster and traces the outlines with an awl.
Fresco painting calls for great skill and experience. Painters know that the colours applied to the damp plaster will look different once the plaster dries. They must also be very sure to completely finish the projected day's work – there is no chance to touch it up later. Moreover, not all pigments can be used on fresh plaster, as can be seen in the glossary on page 19. Some paints must be applied 'dry', bound to the plaster by a sort of glue called 'tempera'. These types of paint are more fragile and over the years may peel off. Instead, true fresco painting is very tough and is therefore also used on external walls. In certain cases, in order to preserve a fresco, it must be detached from the wall. This operation may reveal the underlying sinopia, as can be seen in the illustrations on page 7.
A fitting conclusion to this work can be drawn from the words of Giorgio Vasari, the great Renaissance artist and writer, who of all painting techniques, judged that frescoing was "the most masterful, the surest, the most resolute and durable of all the others."

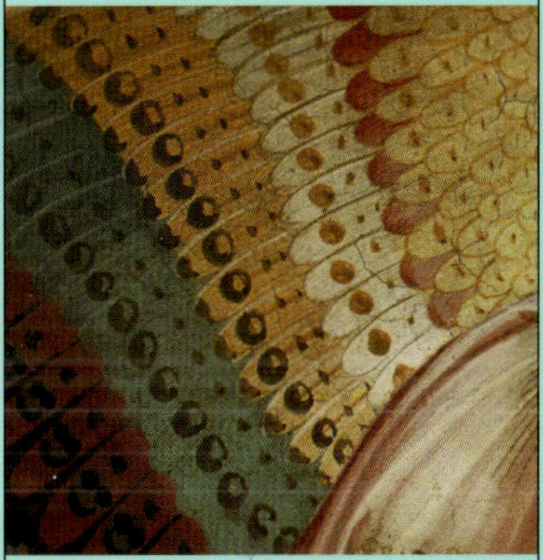

ISBN 88-8347-302-7

9 788883 473029

€ 4,50

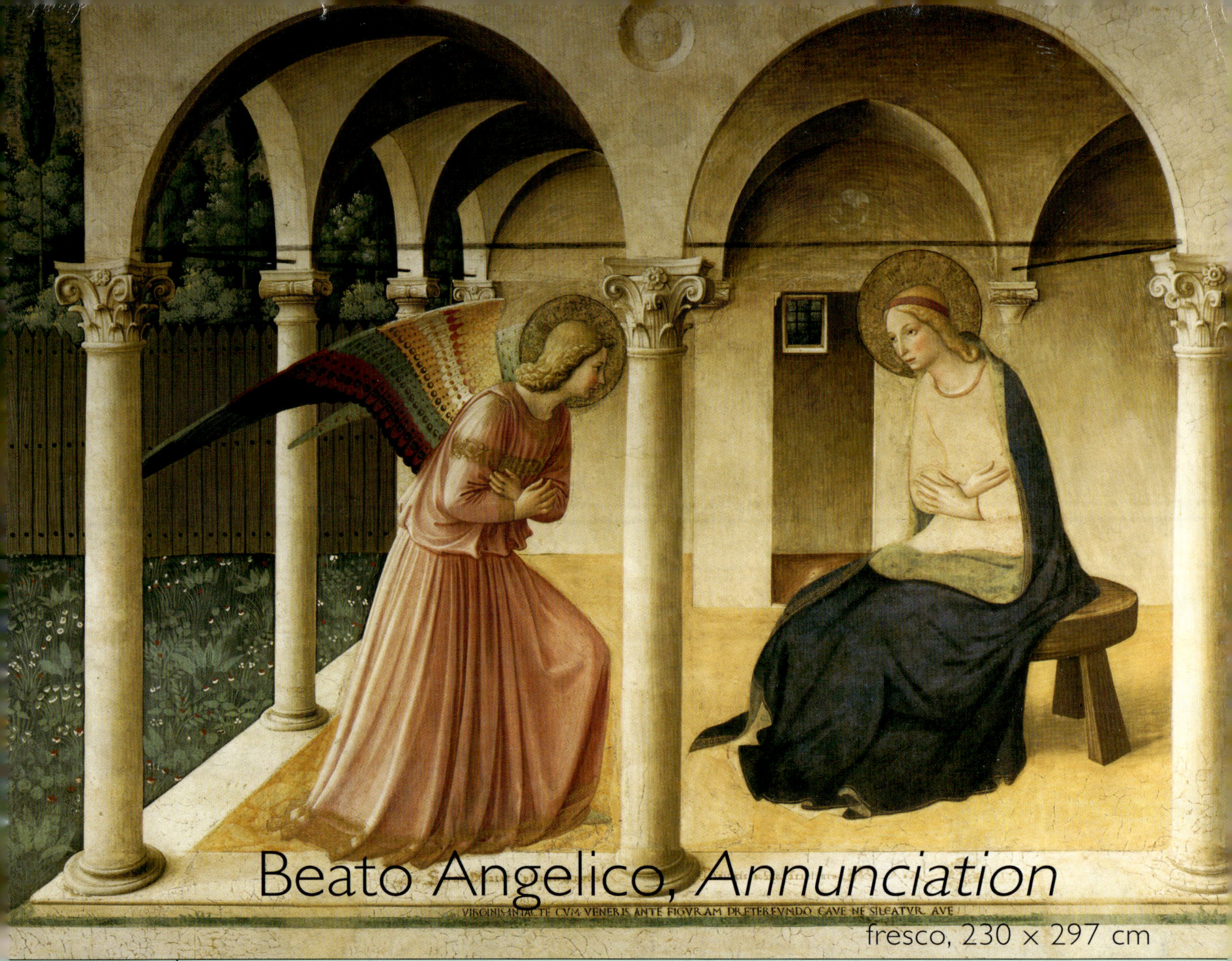


Beato Angelico, *Annunciation*

fresco, 230 × 297 cm

## TO LEARN MORE


Cennino Cennini, *Il libro dell'arte* (*The Book of Art*), edited by Fabio Frezzato, Vicenza 2003

Giorgio Vasari, *Le vite de' più eccellenti pittori scultori e architettori* (*The lives of the most excellent painters, sculptors and architects*; 1568), edited by G. Milanesi, vol. I, Florence 1878, various editions

Ugo Procacci, Lucio Guarnieri, *Come nasce un affresco*, Florence 1975

Giorgio Bonsanti, *Gli affreschi del Beato Angelico*, in *La chiesa e il convento di San Marco a Firenze*, Florence 1990, vol. II, pp. 115-172

Magnolia Scudieri, *Gli affreschi di San Marco nella storia del restauro*, in *Le pitture murali*, Florence 1990, pp. 269-292

Daniela Dini, *Gli affreschi del Beato Angelico nel Convento di San Marco a Firenze: rilettura di un capolavoro attraverso un memorabile restauro*, Turin 1996

Magnolia Scudieri, *Gli affreschi dell'Angelico a San Marco*, Florence-Milan 2004


printed in January 2006
by MediaPrint - Livorno
for
sillabe